A KIDS' GUIDE TO MANNERS

A KIDS' GUIDE TO

MANNERS

50 FUN ETIQUETTE LESSONS FOR KiDS & Their Families

KATHERINE FLANNERY

ILLUSTRATED BY JANE SANDERS

ROCKRIDGE
PRESS

contents

A Letter to Grown-ups

Dear parents, grandparents, teachers, and maybe even some fed-up aunts and uncles,

The world has really moved on since we were kids, huh? Everything is a rush these days, and as the world spins faster, formalities get flung off into space. While it's great that things aren't as chafingly stiff as they once were, there are some etiquette standards and manners practices that remain super important for getting along well in this world. If you know them, they seem like common sense, but really they're a second nature that you have to learn when you're a kid.

This book isn't about resurrecting stodgy old rules to make kids into quiet little automatons (as appealing as that may sound sometimes); it's about the essential manners that will make kids happy, confident, well-functioning global citizens. It's about engaging kids with fun activities that show them how manners will make their lives easier, win them friends, and help them get along with everyone from family members to teachers, to besties to bullies.

You can go through this book with younger children or give it to older kids to read on their own. Either way, the best thing you can do to reinforce the good behavior in this book is, you guessed it, model it yourself. After all, little monkeys see, little monkeys do, so I recommend doing some "Try as a Family" activities with kids.

☺ TRY AS A FAMILY

Everyone wants to give the kids they love a leg up, and teaching them manners does that for life.

Sincerely,

KATHERINE

Writer, Editor, Family-Haver

A Letter
to Kids

HELLO!

Are you ready for your life to get a *lot* easier? You might think that a book on etiquette* would make your life harder. What if it is filled with a bunch of boring rules? Or what if it tries to make you feel bad for being the fun and funny kid you are? Well, you, my friend, are in for a surprise!

The whole reason we have manners is to make life easy and fun. It's true! Manners help us make friends and get along with lots of different people. Manners have a bad reputation for being pointless or hard, but the truth is manners are just ways to be nice to people. And when you're nice to people, they will be nice to you. That's all there is to it!

Part of growing up is learning what to do in lots of situations. Knowing good manners makes doing the right thing as simple as blinking. You just do it without thinking. When you have good manners, you know you're doing the right thing. Manners give you more confidence!

This book is full of great stories and activities to show you that manners really are easy. It will also let you in on the super simple reasons behind manners. Once you know why it's a good idea to do something, it's a cinch to start doing it.

According to the really smart writer and poet Ralph Waldo Emerson, "Manners are the happy way of doing things." Well said, Ralph. That's exactly what manners are. So, go on and explore the easy, happy, and awesome ideas in this book!

Your friend,

KATHERINE

Etiquette is pretty much just a fancy word for manners.

Chapter 1

Why Do Manners Matter?

This chapter is all about why having good manners is a great thing. Once you know why manners are important, it will become oh-so-easy to use them without even thinking about it. Good manners make a lot of sense once you learn about them. They make your life easier and happier. Who doesn't want that?

Why Manners Are Really Great

Y ou might not believe that manners are "great." *Yet!* You might think they're some gooey blob of rules that are hard to figure out. And you might think that calling manners "great" is just the kind of stuff grown-ups say to get kids to behave.

I admit it, I am a grown-up. (At least I am if you just think about my age. If you judge me by my massive dinosaur collection instead, you might think I'm still a kid.) But I promise that manners aren't just some adult nonsense to get you to be quiet and put away your stuff.

Manners really are great because they make you feel great! They make it easy to get along with lots of people. When you have good manners, you'll always know what to do and say. Good manners make life so much easier!

Plus, manners aren't hard to learn. In fact, there's only one thing you need to know to have awesome manners, and it's the same thing that makes manners feel good.

Are you ready for the one big secret to manners?

Having manners just means being kind to people. That's it! It's that simple. Being nice to people feels good. Plus, when you're nice to people, they're almost always nice back. When everyone has good manners, everyone feels good. It's like a snowball that starts small, but the more you roll it, the bigger it gets.

Once you start using this book and try out good manners on your friends and family, you'll find out for yourself just how great they are.

RESPECT

You probably hear this word a lot, but what does "respect" mean? Respect is understanding that other people have feelings—just like you do—and thinking about those feelings. Respect is showing people you appreciate them and value them. Treating someone respectfully means treating that person how they want to be treated. So really it just means being nice!

When you are respectful, people will like you and respect you back. And do you know what happens then? You make lots of friends! Who doesn't want to hang out with the super nice kid?

You can show someone respect in lots of ways, and none of them are hard. Showing respect is as simple as a smile and friendly greeting, saying "please" and "thank you," or sharing your awesome toys and games with friends. There's even more about this in chapter 2.

RESPONSIBILITY

This can feel like a heavy word with lots of not fun things dragging it down. When you hear "responsibility" you might think "chores" or "homework." Woof! Nobody likes that stuff.

I am not going to pretend that acting responsibly by cleaning your room or doing your homework is the best time ever while you're doing it. Usually it's not. But that stuff has to get done, and if you do it when you're supposed to—and without a lot of complaining—you're going to impress the heck out of adults. And when adults are impressed with you, that means big bonuses!

Responsible kids get stuff like pets, later bed times, bigger allowances, and some wiggle room when they mess up. It means . . . getting more of what you want!

GETTING WHAT YOU WANT

You know that having good manners means being kind and considerate of other people. But did you know that there's a totally selfish reason for having good manners? Well, there is. And it's a big one!

When you have good manners, act responsibly, and respect others, people will see how awesome you are. And when people know you're awesome, they're more likely to say "yes" when you ask for something. We're talking parents, siblings, friends, teachers, and even people you've just met. When people like and trust you, you get kindness, respect, freedom, friendship, and more in return.

In short, having good manners gets you what you want!

What Manners Are,
and What Manners Are NOT

Now that you know manners are all about being nice to people, can you figure out what manners are, and what manners are not? From each set of ABCs, pick the one you think means good manners.

A. Manners are only for snobby people.

B. Manners are a way for anyone to show that they're a nice person.

C. Manners are just for adults. Kids don't need them.

A. When I first meet someone I should ignore them, because I don't know if I like them yet.

B. When I meet someone new, I am nice to them, because I like it when people make me feel the same way.

C. When I meet someone new, I should wait for them to be nice to me before I am nice to them.

A. When I go to my best friend's house, I don't say "please" or "thank you" to her family because I see them all the time.

B. When I go to my best friend's house, I say "please" and "thank you" to her family because I like them and want to be polite.

C. When I go to my best friend's house, it's okay if I scream and make a mess, because that's what kids do.

If you answered B to all of the above, you've got a good idea about good manners!

FAMILY CITIZEN

Being a citizen means being a member of a group. To be a good citizen means that you respect your group by listening to the people in it, and by taking care of the things you share with the group.

The very first group that everyone is part of is their family. Being a good family citizen means doing what your family needs you to do. Your parents need you to do your chores. Your siblings need you to have tons of fun. Your pets need you to feed them.

That's a lot of things to take care of! But what you give, you get. Your parents give you everything from food to toys to love. Your siblings will share their toys and adventures with you, if you share yours with them. And your pets will cuddle you like crazy when you take good care of them.

QUICK TIPS FOR BEING A
GREAT FAMILY CITIZEN

Your family will be thrilled if you do these simple things around the house. No one is perfect, and you might not remember to do all these things all the time. But the more you try, the better you'll be!

★ Say hi when you see your family members—don't just run past like they aren't there.

★ Knock on a closed door before going into a room.

★ Don't mess with other people's stuff without asking first.

★ Don't yell for people—go and find them when you want to talk to them.

★ Come to meals as soon as you're asked.

★ Do chores when you're asked (making your parents ask you again and again is downright rude), or even better, before you're asked!

★ Clean up after yourself and put things back where you found them.

★ Keep your voice, your music, and the TV at a volume that doesn't blast through the whole house. Try to keep all that stuff quiet enough that it can't be heard outside the room you're in. Just *try*.

★ Share your toys with your siblings and handle theirs with care.

COMMUNITY CITIZEN

In addition to being citizens of our families, we are citizens of an even larger group: Our community. Our community is made up of all the people around us, like our neighbors, our school, our friends, our church, and even our whole town or city.

You can be an awesome community citizen by treating the people you meet and the places you go with respect. This means being friendly and helpful to your friends, classmates, and all the people you meet. It also means taking care not to litter, make graffiti, or break anything that's not yours. It's easy to be a community citizen when you use good manners!

QUICK TIPS FOR BEING A
GREAT COMMUNITY CITIZEN

**You'll be a star in your community
if you do these easy things:**

★ Give a friendly smile and hello when you see people you know.

★ Pick up litter.

★ Offer to help elderly people cross the street.

★ Hold doors open for people.

★ Use a calm voice and don't run around or shout, especially indoors.

WORLD CITIZEN

It's easy to see that you're an important citizen in your family and community. What you do in those groups matters. But did you know that you're also a citizen of the world? It's true. What you do can impact the whole planet!

It might not seem like just one kid has much of an effect on the world, but when you are friendly and kind to the people around you, that goodness will spread. When you're nice to someone, that puts them in a better mood. Then they're more likely to be nice to the next person they see, who will be nice to the next person they see, who will be nice to the next person they see. It could go on forever!

Making the world a better place really does start with you and something as simple as a friendly smile.

QUICK TIPS FOR BEING A
GREAT WORLD CITIZEN

**Being a cool kid in this big world
is actually pretty easy!**

★ Be friendly and considerate to all people.

★ Give everyone respect, no matter how different they are from you.

★ Recycle.

★ Try not to be wasteful. This means don't waste electricity or food, and don't buy things you don't need.

★ Donate things you no longer use to kids who don't have as many toys and clothes as you.

★ Keep on being the super great kid you are!

SHOWING THE WORLD WHO YOU ARE

Now that you see that what you do affects the people around you—from your friends and family to the whole wide world—it's time to let everyone know what a terrific kid you are. Being a well-mannered citizen who takes care of his or her responsibilities shouts to the world, "I am awesome!" Politely, of course.

The easiest way to show the world how wonderful you are is to make a good first impression. If you're friendly and kind the very first time you meet someone, that person will immediately think, *What a cool kid!* It's a great way to win friends and get people to respect you. As you read this book, you'll find out lots of ways to show the world you're awesome.

Remember, you get what you give.

If you make a bad first impression, people probably won't be excited the next time they see you. And if you want them to like you and be friendly to you, you'll have to work very hard to change their minds about you. So, make it easy on yourself by being your best every time you meet someone. In this book, you'll be learning lots of ways to make a good impression, which means more confidence and fun!

It's All About Kindness

B eing kind is at the very heart of manners. It means doing good things to make other people happy. When you make other people happy, that will make you happy. What could be better?

Good manners are easy shortcuts to have people enjoy being around you. Really, that's what manners are all about! Being kind, respectful, responsible, compassionate, and thoughtful about what other people need—well, that may sound like a lot! But knowing good manners makes all of that stuff so easy that you'll do it without even having to think about it.

Remember, it all boils down to being nice. As long as you're being nice to people, you're showing good manners. When you act respectfully (treating someone the way they like to be treated) and do kind things, you're being the best you can be *and* letting everyone around you see just how awesome you are!

COMPASSION

Compassion is another one of those words that may seem big and hard, but it's super easy: Compassion just means caring about others and their well-being by considering how they feel and wanting them to be happy. Having compassion is a great way to be kind and thoughtful.

When you notice someone else is sad or upset, you can show that you care by trying to cheer them up. For example, you see a classmate looking lonely on the playground. Put yourself in his place. Do you remember ever feeling lonely and wishing someone would come say hi? That's something we've all felt, and it doesn't feel so good, huh?

The compassionate thing to do is to go over and see if you can cheer him up. You could tell him a joke, like "Why shouldn't you play games in the jungle? Too many *cheetahs*!" Or you could ask him to hang out. Making him feel welcome will make him feel better, and you're going to feel great, too.

BEING THOUGHTFUL

Being thoughtful is a lot like being compassionate. It means thinking about how other people feel. But thoughtfulness isn't just being kind when people are upset, it's being kind all the time.

Maybe you see your mom with *that* look in her eyes. You know the one, when she's got a million things to do and no time to do them. Being thoughtful means thinking about how you could help her without her having to ask you for help. If the garbage is full, go ahead and take it out. If you know she's about to run around looking for her keys, go get them for her and put them in a place where she'll definitely see them. And if you aren't sure how to help, you can always ask her what you can do!

Every time you are thoughtful, you'll make someone feel happy and cared for, and you'll feel happy, too. Win-win!

HELPING OTHERS JUST BECAUSE

Helping others "just because" is one of the biggest, best things to make the world a better place. Every single nice thing you do is one more good thing that happens on planet Earth.

Doing something "just because" means you're doing it for no reason other than to be kind. No one asked you to help, and you're not looking to get anything back. You're just helping because you're awesome. End of story!

There are so many ways to help out others just because, which means you can be really creative. If your best friend likes dinosaurs, draw them a picture of their favorite dinosaur. If someone is coming into a building behind you, hold the door open for him or her. Pass your brother his favorite food at dinner before you serve yourself. Donate toys you don't play with anymore. The more "just because" things you do show that you have good manners and make you a cool kid to be around!

DOING GOOD FEELS GOOD

I know I said that helping others just because means doing something kind without expecting anything in return. End of story. While that first part is true, it's not *really* the end of the story.

Even when you help out just because, without wanting to get anything back, you actually *do* get something back automatically—you're going to feel good. Soon, you won't be able to help yourself! Making someone else smile will make you smile. Making someone else happy will make you happy. That's just how it goes.

So, you *do* get something back when you help others. That good feeling isn't *why* you help other people, but it sure is a bonus!

LET'S REVIEW!

Manners can seem like a lot of work, but they are super easy to learn! Look at what you just learned:

★ *Being kind is the start of all good manners. If you can do that, the rest is easy!*

★ *Kids with good manners, who are kind, respectful, and responsible, are way more likely to get what they want.*

★ *Being a citizen means being a member of a group, and being a good citizen means being kind and considerate to your group.*

★ *Making an awesome first impression is one of the many ways to show someone how great you are!*

★ *Compassion is when you care about someone's well-being and want to help them feel happy.*

★ *Doing good for others makes us feel good, too.*

Chapter 2

Manners 101

Hello, and welcome to the basics. This chapter is all about the simplest ways you can start being kind and well-mannered right this very second. You'll find out the best ways to say hi to people. You'll also make sure that when you talk, you say the right things so people will listen. Finally, we'll talk about how to deal with bullies, gossipers, and anybody who isn't treating you with respect. Once you know the basics, talking with just about anybody will be easy-peasy.

Magic Words

You've probably been hearing about the "magic words" forever. You tell your mom you want something, and she asks you, "What's the magic word?" You know she wants to hear "please," but why is that word "magic"?

Please, **thank you**, **you're welcome**, and **excuse me** are all magic phrases because so much greatness is packed inside those little words. They really mean "I think you're cool, I respect you, and I want to be nice to you. I'm also cool, I deserve your respect, and you should treat me nicely, too." Now that's saying a lot by saying a little, which really is a kind of magic!

Saying "please" shows that you understand when you are asking someone to go out of their way to do something for you. Even if you just want your brother to pass the mashed potatoes, a "please" is likely to get you those mashed potatoes instead of getting you a "No way!" or "Get them yourself!"

Saying "thank you" shows you appreciate that someone did something nice for you. Sure, it was just passing the mashed potatoes, but your brother spent his time doing something for you. It's only right for you to send some magic his way.

When someone uses the magic phrases "please" and "thank you" on you, saying "you're welcome" finishes up the magic spell. You did something nice, and they appreciate it. You feel good because they used magic words. Saying "you're welcome" back makes you both feel awesome and appreciated.

"Excuse me" is the totally cool, and totally not rude, way to get someone's attention. If you say "excuse me" to your mom the next time you want to ask her something, trust me, you'll see for yourself just how magical those words are!

PLEASE
thank you
Excuse me
You're welcome!

Greetings

"Hey, what's up?" You probably say that to your friends all the time. That's totally fine! But do you say it to your friends' parents? What about teachers? If you greet adults this way, you've probably gotten some looks that say "not cool."

The way you greet someone says a lot about what you think of that person. "Hey, what's up?" says "I know you. We're buds!" But when you don't know someone, or you are greeting a friend's parents or your teacher, a greeting like that says the wrong thing.

When you are talking to an adult, or even a kid you don't know very well, **hello**, **good morning**, **good afternoon**, and **good evening** say the right thing. They are greetings that show you are kind and know a thing or two about manners. These greetings are also great because the very first thing you say to someone shows that you respect them. That will earn you respect in return. Then you're off to a great start instead of getting a look that says "not cool."

"Hello" will work for anyone at any time of day. Throw in a smile, and you'll show everyone that you're happy to meet them.

"Good morning" is a swell way to say hi before lunch.

If you've already had lunch but you haven't had dinner, "good afternoon" is the way to go.

When it's dinnertime or later, "good evening" is on the menu.

By using hello and the "good" greetings, you'll show people how awesome you are. As a bonus, these little shows of kindness might just make someone's day. (See page 29 to learn more about little ways to make someone's day.)

Communication, Speaking Up, and Expressing Yourself

You probably talk to lots of people every day. Your friends, your family, your teachers, your neighbors, and maybe a coach or a babysitter. Good communication means saying what you mean so that people will listen. Just like with greetings, you can be laid back with your friends, but you should give new people and grown-ups a little extra manners magic.

If you're being mega rude, no one wants to hear that! Not even your friends. If you're being polite, people will almost always be happy to hear what you have to say. Then they will speak to you with the same friendliness and respect.

Let's say you need a trip to the bathroom during class. Saying "Excuse me, may I please go to the bathroom," is sure to go over better than "Hey! I gotta go!"

If you're at your friend's house to play video games and say, "I want to play! Gimme that controller!" that will probably make your friend feel bad. They might even think you're a meanie and not invite you back. If you say, "Can I have the controller after your turn?" then the good times will keep going.

No matter who you are talking to, if you don't like what's happening, it's really important to speak up. If someone is being mean or making you feel uncomfortable, say so. "I don't like the way you're talking to me," and "I don't like that," are perfectly okay things to say.

Having good manners means treating people with respect and getting respect in return. It doesn't mean letting other people get their way even when their way makes you feel bad. If someone still makes you feel bad after you spoke up, it's okay to tell an adult.

Friendship

Let's say Kevin invites Sam over to hang out. When Sam gets there, Kevin doesn't say hi. He just keeps playing with his remote-controlled drone. When Sam asks for a turn, Kevin snorts and says, "You wish." Rude!

When Kevin is done with the drone, he walks into the backyard and Sam follows him. Sam isn't having fun, but he decides to give Kevin another chance. Kevin says he wants to pretend fight with some plastic swords. Sam says, "I don't like sword fighting. Can we play a board game?" Kevin says, "Don't be a baby," and whacks Sam on the head with a plastic sword. That really hurt!

Sam says, "That's not cool! That hurt." Kevin says, "If you don't like it, then leave." So Sam does. If Kevin isn't going to be nice to Sam or treat Sam with respect, why should Sam stay? That's not how friends treat one another.

The next week Mike invites Sam over. When Sam gets there, Mike says, "Hey, Sam! I'm glad you're here. I just got a great new game. Want to play?" Sam says, "Sure!" Mike wasn't lying—it's an awesome game! Then Mike offers Sam a snack and asks what Sam wants to do next. They decide to ride bikes and they have a super fun time.

Sam decides he's not going to go over to Kevin's house anymore. Sam and Mike stay really good friends and hang out all the time.

Friends are fun to be around. They are considerate of what you like and what you want to do, and you treat them the same way. Mike treated Sam like a friend, but Kevin treated Sam like gum stuck to his shoe. Who needs that!?

LITTLE WAYS TO BE KIND   😊 TRY AS A FAMILY

A little kindness goes a long way! Here are some quick things you can do to be a kind kid, or a great goat* if you prefer:

★ Give up your seat on the bus or subway to elderly folks, pregnant people, or someone who looks really tired. You're young and full of zip-bang-zoom! So cut the other folks a break.

★ If a friend is having a bad day, tell him or her some jokes. Did you hear the one about the bear with no teeth? He was a real *gummy* bear!

★ Mom can always use a little help around the house. You'll be the kindest kid on the block if you do a chore before she asks you to do it.

★ Throw out some litter that's near your house (but don't touch anything too gross).

★ Tell your parents you would like to volunteer, maybe at an animal shelter or a soup kitchen. (Okay, this is kind of a big thing, but it's also an amazing thing!)

★ If you have any elderly neighbors, offer to bring them their mail.

★ Go through your stuff and donate the clothes and toys you don't use anymore.

*Get it!? Kids are young goats, so a kind kid and a great goat are sort of the same thing.

LITTLE WAYS TO MAKE SOMEONE'S DAY

I bet you can make someone's day in under ten seconds. That's all it takes! You can:

★ Say hello with a big smile.

★ Invite someone you don't normally play with to join in on a game.

★ Hold the door open for the person behind you.

★ Let someone go ahead of you in line.

★ Call a relative just to say hello.

★ Tell a joke! (This idea should be on all lists, all the time.) You can try "Knock knock. Who's there? An interrupting pirate. An interrupting pi—Yarrrrrrrrrrrr!!!"

★ Pay someone a compliment just because you like them, and everyone likes getting compliments.

★ Tell someone how much you like them.

★ Share your dessert. Everyone loves dessert!

★ Leave a heads-up penny somewhere someone will pick it up.

★ Thank your teacher.

★ Ask a parent about *their* day.

★ Clean up after yourself by putting away anything you use.

★ Chat with a classmate who looks a little lonely.

What If I'm Not Being Treated With Respect?

We all deserve respect. When people are mean, hit or hurt us, or treat us in ways we don't like, we don't have to put up with it. We can tell those people to stop being a meanie, and we can do it without becoming meanies ourselves.

When someone does something rude or disrespectful, a lot of times the first thing we want to do is get them back. But we all know two wrongs don't make a right. Instead of hitting or yelling back, simply say, "That's rude, dude. Please stop doing it." That's usually all it takes to get things back on a good track, especially if it's your friend who is being uncool. He or she might have just gotten carried away. We all go a little over the top sometimes!

When you say stop, at first the person may get upset. He or she may try to pretend it was all a joke and you are making a big deal out of nothing. People do this when they realize they were being uncool and they feel embarrassed about it. That's something we all do sometimes! If a person reacts like that, the best thing to do is keep calm and carry on being considerate. If we keep playing the game or doing whatever we were doing, the bad feelings will blow over fast.

What if the bad behavior is from someone who is *always* mean? Or what if we think someone is really trying to hurt us or make us upset? We're talking about bullies here. Dealing with them stinks! It's a good thing there is a lot we can do to get bullies to buzz off. Keep reading to find out how!

HANDLING BULLIES, GOSSIPS & MEANIES

There are lots of things you can do to stop bullies, gossips, and other meanies:

- ✓ Avoid meanies. Don't waste your time on them.

- ✓ Feel great about being you! That's the best defense against meanies.

- ✓ Stand up for yourself by saying, "No, stop it!" and walking away.

- ✓ If a gossip or a meanie tells you a bad story about another person, tell that meanie you don't want to hear it and walk away.

- ✓ If a meanie just won't quit, hurts you, or makes you feel unsafe, tell an adult right away.

- ✓ If a meanie says some nasty things about another person, try saying something nice about the person they're bad-mouthing and then walk away.

- ✓ If a meanie is spreading gossip about you, ignore it or tell an adult if it's making you uncomfortable.

- ✓ Don't let meanies get to you. If you just act like a cool cucumber, they won't bother with you.

- ✓ Don't be a meanie yourself. If you hit or yell or say nasty things to get back at someone, then you've become the meanie!

- ✓ Don't spread gossip around. Repeating icky stories is something meanies do.

LET'S REVIEW!

You can learn the basics of manners in a snap.

★ *The magic words are greatness packed into little phrases, like a rabbit in a hat!*

★ *Good greetings like "good morning" and "hello" show others you're friendly and that you respect them.*

★ *If someone is a meanie, don't be afraid to speak up, and tell an adult if you need to.*

★ *Don't become a meanie yourself.*

★ *Friends are always considerate and respectful of each other.*

★ *It's easy to be kind or make someone's day!*

Chapter 3

Representing Yourself and Talking to Others

When you first meet someone, sometimes you can feel awkward if you don't know what to do or say. No need to fear—good manners to the rescue! There are a bunch of simple things you can do to make meeting new people fun and talking to them easy-peasy.

Making a Good Impression

You know when you meet someone and you immediately like them? You think, *What a cool kid!* The next time you see that person, you're probably happy about it. That's because they made a good impression on you.

Making a good impression is the first step toward making friends and impressing adults. Good thing it's easy to do! All it takes to make a good impression is to be friendly and respectful. If you seem really happy to meet someone, they'll be happy to meet you, too. If you show them respect, you'll get respect back.

That will put your whole relationship on the fun-and-easy track. That is way better than the annoying-and-rude track, which is where you end up if you make a bad impression. Once you're on that track, you have to work extra hard to prove that you are actually awesome.

There are a few good manners in this chapter that are sure to make a good impression on everyone you meet. You can also look back to Tip #2 (page 24) to brush up on great greetings.

Introducing Yourself and Others

When you meet someone new, give them a friendly smile, a great greeting (see Tip #2, page 24), and your name. "Hello, my name is Betty" is a great start!

Then, if you want, you can add in a little something about yourself. "I'm in Ms. Walker's second grade class at Lanes Mill Elementary."

Now top it off with a little extra niceness. "It's nice to meet you!" This is sure to make an awesome impression on anyone.

Sometimes you'll need to introduce other people. For example, you're at the park with your friend Jim, and hey, here comes Diane! You know Jim and Diane, but they don't know each other. Introducing them is easy.

"Diane, this is Jim. Jim, this is Diane." Saying each person's name twice will help everyone remember the new names.

Just like when you introduce yourself, if you want you can add a little information about the people you're introducing. You can tell Diane, "Jim is a terrific builder. We're making a fort." You can tell Jim, "Diane is in my class, and she's awesome at math."

If you're introducing adults, using their proper names will win you big manners points. (See Tip #8, page 39, for more.)

Using Proper Names and Last Names

You already know that you can be more laid back with other kids than with adults. When you introduce kids to each other, using their first names is completely fine. When you're introducing adults, though, using proper names like Mr., Ms., or Mrs. plus their last names is the well-mannered thing to do.

Here are all the proper names you need to know:

Mr. (mister), which can be used for any man.

Ms. (pronounced mizz, rhymes with fizz), which can be used for any woman.

That's it! Just those two!

The proper names **Mrs.** (missus) and **Miss** are also okay to use. You use "Mrs." for a woman who is married, and "Miss" for a woman who is not. But what if you don't know if someone is married? Or what if the woman doesn't want her proper name to depend on whether or not she's married? Using "Ms." just makes the whole thing easy!

To make a great introduction, tell the people you're introducing a little bit about each other. For example, you're at the supermarket with your mom and you see your gym coach.

"Mom, I'd like you to meet Ms. Mable, my gym coach. She's amazing at dodge ball. Ms. Mable, this is my mom, Mrs. Chang. She played volleyball in college."

Even after you've been introduced to an adult, keep using that person's proper name plus the last name to show good manners and respect. Only call them by their first name if they invite you to. Remember, respect is about treating people the way they want to be treated.

Standing When You Meet Someone

We can all get a little nervous when we meet someone new, but good manners tell us exactly what to do. When we know what to do, meeting people is no problem at all.

A great way we can show someone we're cool and we know about manners is to stand up when we meet them. Standing up when we meet someone shows that person we care about meeting them. It's a way to show respect. It's a way to say, "Oh, sweet, a new person!" without actually saying those words out loud. That might be a little weird!

When we make the little extra effort of standing up to show someone we care, that makes them feel good. When we make someone else feel good, we feel good, too. When everyone is feeling good, then first meetings can lead to more good times!

Eye Contact

When you talk, you want people to pay attention to what you're saying. And the same is true the other way around. When people talk to you, they like to know that you're listening.

Eye contact is when you look someone right in the eyes when you're talking with them. It may feel a little weird at first, but it's the best way to show someone that you really are paying attention to everything they're saying.

In that way, making eye contact shows someone respect, so it's a great thing to do when you first meet someone. It also shows that you have confidence in yourself. No staring at your feet and mumbling for you. You're too confident for that!

Adults will be super impressed if you make eye contact when you introduce yourself. Just try it, and you'll see it's kind of like magic.

Guess what? Eye contact also helps you to actually pay attention when people are talking. If you look someone in the eyes when they're speaking—even if what they're saying is, well, kind of boring—it is easier to keep listening. Instead of drifting off and thinking about robots or squirrels or wondering how you make a tissue dance (you put a little boogie in it!), you will stay interested, and who knows, maybe you will learn something new!

⊙ TRY AS A FAMILY

Handshakes

There is one last secret to great manners when you meet someone. It's the handshake. Oh boy, will people be impressed with you if you shake their hand when you meet them! All you need to do is this:

1. Stick out your right hand (the one that goes over your heart during the Pledge of Allegiance).

2. Squeeze the other person's hand like you would a tube of toothpaste. Not so hard the toothpaste squirts out everywhere, but not so softly that nothing even comes out.

3. Shake your hand (it's a handshake after all!) up and down once or twice.

4. That's it! Handshake accomplished!

Like all the other things you do when you meet people, the handshake is a bit of good manners that shows the other person respect and that you're a great kid.

You can keep using handshakes even after the first time you meet people along with a friendly "hello" and eye contact. These are best used on adults that keep things appropriate and formal.

If you want to take your handshake to the next level, make eye contact with your fellow shaker.

Being On Time

Zara just couldn't get out of bed. She had stayed up writing in her journal way later than she was supposed to. Whoops! She hit the snooze at least five times, but it wasn't until her mom knocked on her door that she finally crawled out from beneath the covers.

"Zara, you're going to miss the bus!"

Never gonna happen, Zara thought. She showered and got dressed, all while her mom kept asking her to speed it up. "Relax!" Zara said as she came down the stairs. Then she saw it. It was the bus, and it was already leaving the bus stop.

Zara's mom was *not* happy. She was going to have to drive Zara to school, which would make her late for work. Her boss was going to be mad at her.

On the drive, Zara's mom asked, "How would you feel if I made you late for a movie with your friends or for soccer practice?" Zara realized her mom never was late for any of those things! That question really made her think.

By sleeping late, Zara was only thinking about herself. She wasn't thinking about how being late would affect the people around her. In this case, she made her mom have a pretty bad day at work.

Zara decided that from then on, she was going to try really hard to always be on time. By doing that, she could show her mom she cares. It would also show everyone around her that she is considerate and respects their time, too.

Getting-to-Know-You

Do you think you know the difference between great questions for conversations, and questions that are conversation enders? Let's find out! Choose the answers you think are the best conversation starters.

A. Do your parents fight?
B. Do you know how much your house is worth?
C. Do you have any brothers or sisters?

A. How much do you weigh?
B. Do you think I'm short?
C. Do you play any sports?

A. How much is your allowance?
B. Does asparagus make your pee smell weird?
C. Do you have any hobbies?

If you answered C to all of the above, you're a conversation champ!

Listening

One of the simplest things you can do to make someone feel respected and important is to listen to them. It's that easy! By paying attention to what someone has to say, you make them feel good, and you can learn a lot about them.

To be a good listener, make eye contact (see Tip #10, page 41). That will help you pay attention.

Ask questions. This will show you're listening, and it will help you understand what the other person is saying.

This next one might sound familiar. Maybe your parents or teacher have said it to you before? Don't interrupt. Even if you have a question, it's rude and mean to cut in while someone is in the middle of a sentence. Wait until they've finished their thought and then ask your question. Who knows, they might even answer your question before they finish!

When someone is done talking, you can show you were listening by making a comment on what they said. Something as simple as "That's so cool! I didn't know some jellyfish glow in the dark" will make the talker feel good. And yes, there really are jellyfish that glow in the dark!

Making Conversation

Antonio and Omar are waiting for the bus. They don't know each other very well. They *could* play on their phones and totally ignore each other. Instead, Antonio says, "Hello, Omar. I like your sneakers."

Omar just got his sneakers and is very excited about them. He says, "Thanks, Antonio! My brother gave them to me for my birthday. I'd wanted them for forever."

Antonio asks, "Oh yeah? When was your birthday? Did you do anything cool?"

Omar answers, "It was just on Wednesday. My parents took me to see the new *Trek Wars* movie. It was awesome!"

Antonio says, "I love *Trek Wars*! It's my favorite series, after *Robotrucks* anyway."

Omar can't believe it; he's having a *Robotrucks*-themed birthday party this weekend! He says, "*Robotrucks* is my favorite, too! I'm even having a *Robotrucks* party this weekend. You should come!"

Antonio was able to go to the party, and he had a fantastic time. That's because the boys had a great conversation!

Making conversation is easy. All it takes is **showing interest** in what the other person has to say. You can do this by **asking questions** and **sharing your own thoughts**. **Taking turns** talking (instead of interrupting each other) will make the conversation as smooth as your favorite slide.

By making conversations you can make friends, learn new things, and maybe even get invited to a party!

Ask Questions

Questions are very important for having a good conversation, especially when we first meet people or are getting to know them. Questions show we are interested in the other person, and they help us learn about other people.

Some fun things to ask about are sports, hobbies, and favorite movies. We can also ask if they have any pets and find out what their favorite subjects are at school. When we ask people about these things, we can find out what we have in common and maybe make a new friend!

We don't want to get too personal though. Asking people we've just met about problems, body stuff, or money can make them uncomfortable. Saying "I had the worst belches last night. Does that ever happen to you?" may help us learn something about a person, but that person may not want to keep talking to us. Also, TMI!

Patience and Understanding

Everyone has their own way of doing things. Your family might eat pizza and play board games every Friday night. (That sounds great! Can I come?) Your friends' families might have tamales and go to the movies, or they might not use any electronic devices and spend Friday nights in prayer.

When you find out someone does things in a different way than you do, your first thought might be *That's wrong!* Or you might think your way of doing things is better. But different doesn't mean it's wrong or worse. It's just different.

It might take you a little while to get used to things that are different. But having a little patience and being willing to understand the world around you helps you get along with lots of people. Plus, once you get used to the idea that your way isn't the only way to do things, it can be fun and exciting to learn about all the different ways people spend their Friday nights!

LIKE ...um

you know...

Like, Um, Toss Out Those Junk Words!

It's like so easy, you know, to, um, like, use junk words, uh, like over and over and over again. Junk words are easy to say, but when you use a lot of them, it's hard for people to understand what you're saying. Just like that first sentence in bold is hard to read! Junk words such as "like" and "um" are words that don't really mean anything, but we say them instead of pausing to think while we're talking. And once we start using them, they quickly become habits.

If you're in the habit of saying "like" and "um" or "you know" or "errrrm" or "gurgle" or whatever, you can kick that habit by slowing down when you talk. Think about what you're saying, and just pause—don't say anything—while you think about your next word.

secrets

Everyone has some secret stuff they don't want the whole world to know about. Secrets can be about all sorts of things, and not all secrets are bad. For example, your sister's birthday is coming up and you know your parents are getting her a bike. That's a great secret to keep! Even if you're a little jealous.

Some secrets are embarrassing. If your best friend tells you she is afraid of clowns, and she asks you to keep it secret because she feels silly about it, that's definitely a secret to keep. Plus, clowns can be really creepy!

Keeping secrets like these is important. No one gets hurt if you keep these secrets, but people would get upset if you blabbed about them. Plus, this continues what we've already talked about: give respect to get respect. You wouldn't want your friend telling the whole playground one of your secrets, right?

But there are some secrets you should not keep. If your best friend says she is being hit by a bully but you should keep it a secret because she's embarrassed, that's not a secret you should keep. She's getting hurt, and secrets about people getting hurt are never okay to keep. Go with her to talk to an adult you both trust. If she won't go, you can tell her that you'll tell an adult you both trust for her.

Just like with a secret about someone getting hurt, if a secret makes you feel uncomfortable, then it is also not a secret you should keep.

If you know a secret about yourself or anyone else and you don't think you should keep it, don't blab about it on the bus. Don't go around telling everyone you know either. Go to an adult you trust and tell them.

Rumors and Gossip

Laura told Mark who told Carlos who told Jessica that Connie cheats on all her science tests, and that's the only reason she always gets As.

Connie actually gets As because she loves science and always studies. Some kids know that, and some don't, but that doesn't stop the rumor from flying around. At recess, a bunch of kids chant "cheater" at Connie.

Connie is so upset that night she can't focus on studying. The lesson is about the life cycle of frogs, which are her favorite, but she can't keep her mind on tadpole tails or fly-catching tongues. Connie only gets a C on the quiz the next day. Bummer!

Rumors and gossip are usually made up, and they're always icky. Whether they are true or not doesn't matter. It's not just bad manners to spread rumors and gossip, it's a meanie move.

When you hear a story about someone else, imagine that story is about you. If you'd want everyone to know the story—like how you won the long-jump contest—then go ahead and spread the exciting news. If you'd rather no one knew the story—like how you fell on your rear end at the long-jump contest—then let the story stop with you.

Dealing With Conflict

No matter how great our manners are, getting into arguments can happen. We can be on our very best behavior and still accidentally crash into someone in the hall or say something that comes across as mean.

When we find ourselves in conflict with other people or when we don't agree, we have to choose which road we want to go down.

First, there's the **high road**. On the high road, we apologize if we hurt someone—even if we didn't mean to hurt them. If the other person gets super angry and calls us names, we walk away.

Second, there's the **low road**. On the low road, we don't apologize, there is lots of yelling, and we do some name-calling of our own.

The low road may seem like the easier road. We don't have to say we're sorry, and we can let out our anger. The problem with the low road is nothing ever gets solved there. Everyone is mad and mean, which feels pretty awful.

The high road is called the "high road" because it takes work to climb up there. But, wow, is it worth it! It might be hard to say "sorry" if we didn't mean to be mean. And it can be *really* tough not to call someone a goober-filled toad when they just called you a slimy beaver butt. But when we try our best to always act with kindness and understanding, fights get solved, and we end up feeling great about ourselves and how we treat others. It's worth the climb!

Rude Words

Other words that you should take out to the curb with the junk are rude words. Saying rude words makes people not want to listen to you. When people don't like listening to you, they won't like helping you or hanging out with you either. Here is a list of bad, rude words and the well-mannered words you can replace them with.

SO RUDE!	SO POLITE!
✗ Hey!	✔ Hello!
✗ Gimme that!	✔ May I please have that?
✗ Shut up!	✔ I don't like what you're saying.
✗ Any curse words	✔ Dang! or Phooey! or Fudge nuggets! or Sugar cookies!

This week, try to notice how often people use junk words and rude words. That includes you! When you start paying attention, you'll probably be surprised how many times you, and even grown-ups, say "uh," "um," and "like." Once you notice how often these words get thrown around, you'll get sick of hearing them. That's the best first step to kicking them to the curb!

LET'S REVIEW

When it comes to showing the world the best version of you, put all your good manners to work:

★ *Be on time, make introductions if you can, shake his or her hand, make eye contact, ask questions, and take turns talking. Don't interrupt!*

★ *If someone does something different than you do, that doesn't mean it's bad. It could be very interesting!*

★ *Keep secrets to yourself, unless they can be harmful.*

★ *Don't spread or start rumors, and take the high road. It's worth it!*

Chapter 4

Dining

What are all those forks for? Why does my napkin look like a swan? Do I have to eat that!?

It might seem like there are a million pointless rules about eating or dining. But you're going to find out that dining manners actually make eating easier! Once you know why we have dining manners in the first place, all the mysteries of the dinner table will be solved.

Table Manners

This chapter will tell you everything you need to know about table manners. To kick it off, let's go over the very basics. Whether you're at the fanciest-schmanciest restaurant in town or sitting down to eat at home, there are a few things you should always do to have a great meal.

Don't bring your phone or other electronics to the table.

Burping and picking food from your teeth is gross to the max. If you feel the urge for either coming on, excuse yourself from the table.

Take small bites and chew with your mouth closed. No one wants to see your half-chewed food, dude!

On that note, wait to talk until after you're done chewing, even if your sister is telling a joke and asks you what a fake noodle is called (an *impasta!*).

These manners may all seem very different, but they are all related. Table manners are about being nice to others—and being nice to be around. When you're at the table, you're hanging out with friends and family. If you pay attention to them (instead of your phone or tablet) you can have a terrific time. And if you don't do gross things, everyone else will have a fun time, too!

POP QUIZ!

Table Manners

Before we dig into the main course on table manners, let's see what you already know. Can you pick the good-manners moves below?

You are SOOOOOO hungry. You get to the table first, and there's a big bowl of your favorite food sitting right there. You:

A. Shovel some onto your plate and dig in!

B. Sneak a couple bites. No one will notice.

C. Wait until everyone is seated so you can enjoy it together. It's Mom's favorite, too!

You're at a restaurant and there's a fancy napkin on your plate. You:

A. Put it next to your plate.

B. Sit on it.

C. Put it on your lap.

You're at your friend's house for dinner, and they're serving something that looks weird or different. You:

A. Say, "That's gross! I'm going to go home for dinner."

B. Push it around on your plate and hope no one notices you haven't actually eaten anything.

C. Eat it anyway. Who knows? Maybe you'll actually like it.

If you answered C for all of these, you're already on the road to great table manners!

Waiting Until Everyone Has Been Served

Sometimes we are so hungry it feels like we are going to keel over if we don't eat RIGHT NOW. We might want to start wolfing down food as soon as it hits our plate. If we give in to that wolf-y craving, our actions are shouting "me first!" and "gimme!" Not a good move.

Good table manners mean waiting to eat until everyone at the table has been served. It's a simple way to show respect and consideration. When we do this, everyone feels like they are sharing the meal.

Coming to the table the first time we're called is another great way to show you care about sharing a meal with your family. Someone worked hard to get that food on the table, and the least we can do is show up on time to eat it. Plus, the food will still be hot, and you will get to eat sooner. Win-win-win!

Elbows Off the Table, Napkin in the Lap

Why is it such a big deal to put your elbows on the table? It's comfortable to rest them there, so why not do it? The manners police might tell you not to do it because it makes you look bored. And looking bored means being rude. That might be true, but there's another really good reason.

If you put your elbows on the table, you might accidentally stick them in some spilled sauce or wandering gravy. Embarrassing! You might also invade the space of the person next to you, or accidentally knock your fork onto the floor.

Putting your napkin in your lap is another way to stop sauce from getting on your clothes. Let the napkin catch all your crumbs and drips so your pants or skirt doesn't have to.

If you need to excuse yourself from the table, just leave your napkin on your chair until you get back. Easy-peasy.

What Do I Do With All These Forks and Spoons?

You're at a restaurant. You want to impress everyone with your manners and look like you know what you're doing. You sit down in your chair. You unfold your napkin and put it in your lap. Then you see them. All those forks! So many spoons! What are they all for? Should you stab a roll with one of them? Spoon out pepper for everyone at the table? That doesn't seem right . . .

Relax. Using all those utensils is actually really easy. The only thing you need to do is start on the outside and work your way in. It's as simple as that! As long as you don't try to eat peas with your butter knife, that is.

The fork all the way on the outside is for your salad, which will be the first thing served. The bigger fork next to it is for your main meal.

The big spoon on the outside is for soup. The littler one next to it is for tea, which will be served later with dessert. Mmmmm! Dessert!

The big knife next to your dinner plate is for, you guessed it, your dinner.

It's that easy!

Formal Dinner Place Setting

If you go to a fancy restaurant or a big event like a wedding, you might get a formal place setting. Don't let "formal" scare you. You use the utensils here the same way you always do, starting on the outside and working your way in. Formal place settings just give you a few extras.

A little knife on a little plate is for buttering bread. You also get to keep your bread on that cute little plate.

If there is a really tiny fork near your spoons that means some yummy seafood is on the menu. You use that little fork for taking the good stuff out of clams, lobster, mussels, and other seafood.

A little fork and spoon at the top of your plate are meant for dessert. Just remember you top a dinner off with dessert, and you'll never forget what to do with those.

Get some practice with formal place settings by offering to set your dinner table at home as if you were at a fancy restaurant. You might not have all the little plates and utensils that restaurants have, but you can pretend, using whatever you do have. No cloth napkins? Use paper towels. No tiny seafood forks? Just put a toothpick in their place. Your parents probably aren't serving lobster anyway, and they'll be super impressed!

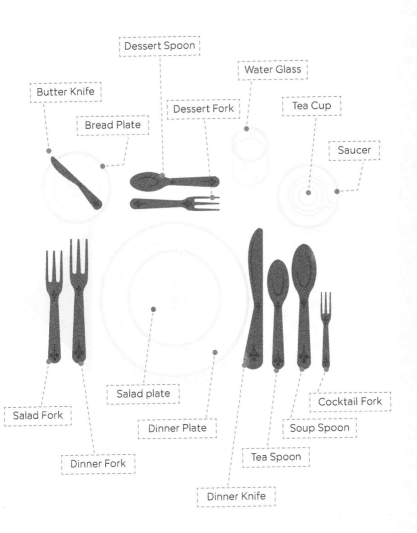

Dessert Spoon

Water Glass

Butter Knife

Tea Cup

Dessert Fork

Bread Plate

Saucer

Salad plate

Salad Fork

Cocktail Fork

Dinner Plate

Soup Spoon

Dinner Fork

Tea Spoon

Dinner Knife

Eating With Fingers, Forks, and Knives

Now that you know what all those utensils are for, don't forget to use them! There are some foods that are okay to eat with your fingers. Chicken nuggets, pizza, and mozzarella sticks are all tasty finger foods. (Is anyone else getting hungry?)

But most foods call for a fork and knife.

When you're eating with a fork, try not to grab it with your whole fist. Instead, hold it in your right hand pretty much the same way you hold a pencil.

When you're cutting food, hold your fork in your left and jab it—gently!—into the food you want to cut. Hold the knife in your right hand. Lay your pointer finger along the top to help control it. Now cut the food by moving the knife back and forth. Cut as gently as you can. If you do it too hard, food might start flying!

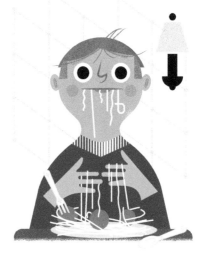

FOOD WARS! FINGERS VS. FORKS

Here's a handy list to help you remember foods you eat with your fingers and foods that use utensils.

Finger Foods

- Nachos

- Pizza

- Sandwiches

- Buffalo wings

- French fries

- Mozzarella sticks

- Anything between two slices of bread

- Anything on a cracker

- Anything with a toothpick stuck in it

Fork Foods

- Spaghetti

- Salad

- Fish (unless it's a fish stick)

- Baked potato

- Chicken breast

- Cooked vegetables

- Cake

- Pork chops

- Burritos that are way too messy to pick up

Please Pass the Pasta

☺ TRY AS A FAMILY

When you sit down to dinner at home or a friend's house, usually all the food is in the middle of the table. Sometimes one person will be in charge of dishing out the food. Other times the food will get passed around and people serve themselves. This is great because you can choose how much food you want.

If you're at a meal where food is being passed around, let someone else be the first person to dig in. That way you don't accidentally start before everyone is ready.

Once people start serving themselves, you can take some food from the dish closest to you. When you're done, pass it to the right. If everyone passes to the right, there won't be any traffic jams at the table.

If it's a heavy dish, you can be a super-awesome guest by holding it for the person to the right as he or she takes food.

If there's something you really want, wait for it to come your way. If it stops at the other side of the table, and no one is passing it, you can say, "Please pass the spaghetti." This only works if it's spaghetti though. If you're waiting for the chicken and say, "Please pass the spaghetti" all you'll get is strange looks.

Many families say a prayer before they eat, but not all families say the same prayer. If you're at someone else's house, and they say a prayer you don't know, you can politely bow your head until it's over.

DOs & DON'Ts > TABLE MANNERS

Here's a quick list to help you remember top-notch table manners.

✔ **DO** Say "excuse me" if you want to leave the table for any reason.

✔ **DO** Say "please" and "thank you."

✔ **DO** Finish everything on your plate, or try your very best.

✔ **DO** Ask politely for another helping if you're still hungry.

✔ **DO** Have a fun conversation and ask questions, too.

✔ **DO** Help clean up.

★ ★ ★

✗ **DON'T** Burp or pick your teeth.

✗ **DON'T** Put your elbows on the table.

✗ **DON'T** Complain about the food or pick around it.

✗ **DON'T** Take the last helping without asking if anyone else wants it.

✗ **DON'T** Talk about gross stuff.

✗ **DON'T** Run off without offering to help clean up.

What If I Don't Like the Food?

Meera is hanging out at her new friend's house. Her friend invites her to stay for dinner and Meera is really excited to accept. Everyone sits down around the table, and her friend's dad puts down a giant pot of chili.

Ugh! Meera hates chili! Ground beef is not her thing. She starts to panic a little bit, but she takes a deep breath. Meera knows this does not have to be a big deal.

When her friend's dad serves her the chili, Meera says, "Thank you." It would be rude to say "no thanks" when she was invited to dinner! Meera focuses on the beans in the chili. They're actually yummy. She tries the ground beef, and she doesn't really like it. For the most part she eats around it, and that's okay. She also makes sure some bites are mostly beans with only a little bit of beef. That way she doesn't leave a big pile of uneaten food on her plate.

By the end of the meal, Meera has eaten a lot of her food. After all, eating something you don't like isn't the end of the world. Meera did the well-mannered thing by eating what she could and not complaining or making grossed-out noises. She and her new friend stay good friends. And luckily there was ice cream for dessert!

Table Conversation

The table is a great place to hang out with your friends and family. They're your favorite people, so make the most of your table time together.

There are lots of conversations you can have at the table. You can just catch up. Find out how your mom's day was. Ask your sister how her model spaceship is coming along.

You can also find out some pretty interesting things. Ask your dad if he has any hidden talents. Ask your sister what she'd do first if she could go to Mars.

But there are some conversations that you shouldn't bring to the table. Body functions? No way. Complaints about the food? Keep them to yourself. Complaints and whining in general. Not good table talk. Name calling. Absolutely not. In fact, that goes for anywhere! Not just the table.

Remember, meals can be fun if you come to the table with a smile and maybe even a silly story. If you show up with a big frown, you're going to bring everybody down, including you!

Another Helping?

Pizza is your all-time, number one, most favorite food. If you could eat one thing every day for the rest of your life, it would definitely be pizza.

Lucky for you, pizza is on the menu tonight! Your mom orders it with your favorite toppings: pineapple and black olives. You get two slices to start, and they are DELICIOUS! You finish them before anyone else finishes theirs. You could still eat more. There's only one slice left though. What do you do?

★ ★ ★

There's nothing wrong with wanting another helping. You're a growing kid after all! But before you take that second helping, make sure everyone else has had a first helping. You don't want to take more if some people have had none.

If there's plenty left, simply ask, "Can I please have another helping?" With such good manners, you're sure to get one.

If there's just a little bit left, like that one last slice of pizza, ask, "Does anyone else want that last piece?" It might be hard to do that. You want that last slice so badly! But being considerate and kind is even better than pizza. Yes, I'm being serious!

Eating Out

Whether you're at a fancy French restaurant or your favorite pizza place, there are a few things you can always do to show what excellent manners you have.

Keep cool as you're walking to your table. If you pick this moment to argue with your brother about who's a better kickball player, the whole restaurant will see it.

Figure out what you want to eat before the server comes to take your order. When the server gets to your table, don't shout out what you want, no matter how excited you are to order it. Let adults order first. Then when the server looks at you, that's how you know it's your turn to order.

Stay in your seat and out of the path between tables. Servers are carrying a lot of heavy trays full of hot, messy food. You don't want to be the cause of an accident!

Remember that you're in a room with lots of other people. That means talking instead of shouting. You don't want everyone in the restaurant to hear what you're saying. By showing everyone what a great kid you are, you will get to go out to dinner more often and that can lead to lots of tasty food!

Splitting a Bill With Friends

Josh, Daniel, and Alexis decide to get some food at the diner on Main Street. Josh orders a milk shake, a burger, cheese fries, and apple pie for dessert. Daniel gets a gyro and a soda. Alexis decides she wants a meatball sub for her meal, ice cream for dessert, and just water to drink.

The bill comes, and Josh says, "Let's just split it three ways." Easy for you to say, Josh! You got way more food than everyone else.

Splitting the bill evenly isn't fair in this case. Daniel doesn't want to make Josh feel bad, but he knows that each person should figure out how much their food costs, and pay that amount. He decides to say, "I'd rather pay for my meal than split the bill." That's all he has to do!

If the three of them had all ordered similar things, then splitting the bill evenly would have been okay. When you're out with friends, try to think about who ordered what when the bill comes to decide how to split the bill.

When the bill comes, you can flex your math muscles to figure out how much you should pay, or ask the server for separate checks when you order your food. It can be easy to figure out the bill when you know what to do!

Tipping

A tip is a little bit of extra money you leave for your server after a meal. It's a way to say, "Thank you! That was great!"

Tipping means math, and for some of us (me!) that can be scary. Luckily, most people have calculators on their phones. You can even download apps that tell you how much a tip should be.

If your server was good, you should leave them a tip that is 20% of the bill. If they were just okay, then you should leave them 15% of the bill.

To figure out how much a tip is, enter the amount of the bill on your calculator. Then multiply that number by .2 for a 20% tip, or .15 for a 15% tip. The number that pops up is how much the tip should be. Add that amount to the total on the bill and you're all set!

Guest Check

Eggs 3.00
bacon 2.00
Milk 1.50
toast 1.00
1.00
Thank You 8.50

Please add 20% Gratuity

LET'S REVIEW!

Table manners help you to be an outstanding kid, whether you're at home or out to eat.

★ *Wait until everyone has been served before digging in.*

★ *Don't fret over table settings! Work your way from the outside toward your plate.*

★ *When food is passed around, pass to the right and help the person next to you with heavy dishes.*

★ *If the meal isn't your favorite, don't complain or say "eww!" Give it a try!*

★ *When you're out with friends, decide how to split the bill fairly and have your calculator ready for the tip.*

Chapter 5

Phones, Devices, and Other Technology

Manners have been around for hundreds, if not thousands, of years. The technology you take with you everywhere you go has only been around for about twenty years. That means the rules about it are pretty new. Good thing you can learn these in a pinch!

Cell Phones and Tablets

Cell phones and tablets are great! They are packed with tons of amazing and useful apps, and you can take them everywhere you go. But just because you have one with you doesn't mean you should always be on it.

If you need to make or take a call, don't make it the main event for everyone around you. Excuse yourself and go to another room or off to the side. Talk in a normal voice. TRUST ME, YOU DON'T NEED TO SHOUT FOR THE OTHER PERSON TO HEAR YOU!

When you're with a group of people hanging out or having a meal, that's not the time to play Angry Candy. It's always better to pay attention to the people you're with than to a screen. That means set your device to silent and put it away. If you forget and it rings, pings, or dings, don't interrupt a real-life conversation to check what's going on.

If you want to take a picture, make sure you ask everyone who will be in the picture if it's okay. Then, if you want to put it online, show it to everyone in it before you post. Just because you think Derek's half-closed eyes and goofy smile look hilarious doesn't mean he will agree! If you're out and about with people, enjoy that time together, not on your device.

Anytime you're in public—the movies, a library, restaurants— make sure you turn the sound on your device off. That means button noises AND the ringer. Better yet, turn the device off completely.

Talking on the Phone

Whether you're on your cell phone or the house phone, good phone manners are always the same.

Answer with a good greeting (see Tip #2, page 24). Before you hang up, say, "Goodbye!"

If you don't know who is calling, ask, "May I ask who's calling?" or "Who is this please?"

Once you know who it is, ask, "Who would you like to talk to?" Then go and get the person the caller would like to talk to. The key is to go and get them. Do not yell at the top of your lungs for them. No one wants to hear that!

If the caller wants to talk to someone who can't come to the phone or isn't home, say, "I'm sorry, he/she can't come to the phone. Can I take a message?" Then write that message down. Don't ever tell a caller you're home alone.

If you don't know the caller, but they still want to talk to you, politely excuse yourself by saying, "Thank you for calling. I have to go. Goodbye." You don't have to answer any questions they ask.

If you do know the caller, follow Tip #14, page 48, to have a great conversation. If your brain goes blank and you don't know what to say, just ask the person how their day is going. That will cut any long, awkward pauses short! See, you already know what to do!

Texting

Text messages seem like they come and go super quickly. But really, text messages can stick around for a really long time. Anything you text to someone, including pictures, can be saved . . . and shared!

A great rule is, don't text anything you wouldn't want your parents to see.

Texting is perfect for public places where talking on the phone would be rude. That doesn't mean you should spend hours with your face glued to the screen. When you're out with your family or friends, remember to pay more attention to them instead of someone on the other end of your texts. And keep the sound on silent!

Texts are best when they're short. And even though they're pretty informal, checking your spelling is still a good idea. Especially because autocorrect thinks it knows what you want to say, even when it doesn't! Correct spelling makes you look smart. Bad spelling mite meen peeple kant undrstandk u.

ALL CAPS AND LOTS OF PUNCTUATION MAKES IT SOUND LIKE YOU ARE SCREAMING!!!!!!!!!!!!!!!! Think about whether or not your message deserves all that yelling.

Not everyone knows what "ROFLMHOBCMDDF" means. Keep the person you're texting in mind when using acronyms and slang.

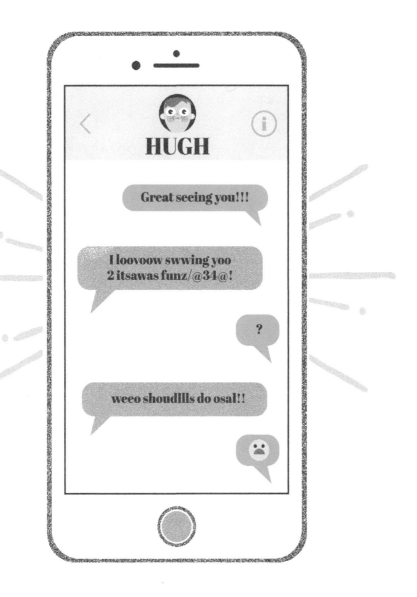

Do you ever get tongue-tied? Or text-tied? If you sometimes don't know what to say on the phone or while texting, here are some well-mannered examples for making good conversation. Or at least dealing with awkward ones!

When Someone Calls but Doesn't Start Talking Right Away

The phone: Ring, ring ring. Ring, ring, ring.

Max: "Hello."

The caller: "Hi."

Max: "Who is calling please?"

The caller: "This is Jodi."

Max: "Good afternoon, Jodi. Who would you like to talk to?"

Jodi, the caller: "Max."

Max: "This is Max."

Jodi: (Total silence—awkward!)

Max: "Can I ask why you're calling?"

Jodi: "My brother is in your class. He's sick and asked me to call to get the homework assignment."

Mystery solved! Now the conversation can go smoothly.

When Someone Calls but Doesn't Stop Talking

The phone: Ring, ring ring. Ring, ring, ring.

Max: "Hello."

Aunt Dottie: "Hi, Max! It's Aunt Dottie. From Michigan. You remember that time I came over for the holidays and brought my little dog, Tiny, and he wee-weed on your new pillow and you didn't know until you put your head on it? That was so funny! We'll have to spend the holidays together again sometime. This past holiday your Uncle Mike and I went to visit friends in Pennsylvania . . ."

Max doesn't want to interrupt, so he waits for Aunt Dottie to take a breath. She'll have to breathe sometime! When she finally does, Max says, "It's nice to hear from you, Aunt Dottie. I bet you want to talk to Mom. Let me get her for you. Hold on please."

Getting a Text from One Friend While You're Hanging Out with a Different Friend

Mike: "Hey, what's up?"

Max: "Hi! I'm hanging out at Jose's house. Is it OK if I text you later?"

Mike: "But I'm SOOOOOOO bored!!!!!"

Max: "Sorry, dude. I'll message you when I get home. Maybe you could check out that new Robotrucks movie? TTYL."

Getting a Text from a Stranger

Texter: "Hi, Max! What are you up to?"

Max: "Hello. Who is this?"

Texter: "Your friend from school!"

Max: "Sorry, I don't know who this is."

That was fishy! If someone won't tell you their name, or if you're not sure who is texting you, block the number and show the texts to your parents.

E-mail Etiquette

Subject: E-mail Etiquette
From: K. Flannery
Date: April 17
To: readers@emailaddress.com

Dear Reader,

E-mails are a lot like conversations. They start with a greeting. If you're e-mailing with your friends, you can be casual. Greetings like "Hey" and slang like "S'up?" are totally okay to use. Basically, you can write like you talk.

If you're e-mailing a kid you don't know very well or an adult, such as a teacher or coach, make sure you show off your good manners. Start with "Dear" or "Hello." Include an adult's proper name and their last name. "Dear Mr. Douglass" is a fine way to start an e-mail. If you're e-mailing an adult you know pretty well who has asked you to call them by their first name, it's okay to use their first name and start your e-mail with Dear Evan or Hello Karen. (When in doubt, use what you learned about greetings in Lesson #2, page 24— these can be applied to any situation.)

Spelling and grammar matters, even with your friends. Writing well helps people understand you. If your e-mails are full of typos and mistakes, they'll be hard to read.

Always end an e-mail with a closing line and your name on the next line. For your friends, you can say "Later" or "Peace." For adults and kids you don't know well, "Sincerely" or "Best" will show you're an e-mail pro.

Sincerely,
Katherine

Spellcheck and Grammar

Correct spelling and good grammar are very important in e-mails and text messages. By making sure we have both, we are making sure everyone can understand what we say. People will know we took time writing to them, which will make them feel good. A well-written message also makes us look smart and impressive. Bonus!

When we write messages really fast and don't bother to check them, those messages are usually full of errors. That means people will have to work very hard to read them. Now that is kind of rude!

Spellcheck is *incredible*. We don't have to spell anything wrong—ever! Most spellchecks are so smart, they even know the difference between "there," "they're," and "their." Even some adults get that confused!

We can check spellcheck before we send an e-mail or text by looking for that little red squiggle. It shows when somehing is wrong. Tapping it or clicking it will usually show the correct spelling.

Grammar takes a little more work. Keep sentences short and to the point. The shorter the sentence, the easier it is to check if the grammar is right.

Using ALL CAPS AND LOTS OF EXCLAMATION POINTS!!!! is not just bad grammar, it also leads to lots of errors. No punctuation and no capitalization also make messages hard to read people will get really confused not being able to read someones messages that is so annoying

Acronyms like "LOL" and "TTYL" would probably get you arrested by the grammar police. That doesn't mean we can never use them. They are okay in casual messages to friends and close family. Make sure the person on the other end will understand them. And we should make sure we don't go overboard with them. OK? G2G. TTFN!

POP QUIZ!

Spellcheck & Grammar

Can you pick out the messages that are spelled correctly and use good grammar?

A. Hello! How's it going? Are we on for the movies tonight?

B. hello how's it going r we on 4 the movies 2nite

C. HELLO!!!!! HOWS IT GONG!?!?!?!? WE GOIN TO TEH MOVIES TONGIGHT????

A. Do you know what pages we need to study for the quiz tomorrow?

B. do u no wut pgs w R suppsd to study 4 teh quiz 2mrow

C. DO YOU KNOW WHAT PAGES WE NEED TO STUDY FOR TOMORROW!?!??!?!?!??!?!

A. I can't wait for the party this weekend! A few people are sleeping over at my house after. Are you in?

B. i cant wait 4 the party this weekend a few people are sleeping over at my house after are you in

C. I CANT WAIT FOR THE PARTY THIS WEEKEND!!!!!!!!!!!!!!! A FEW PEOPLE ARE SLEEPING OVER AT MY HOUSE AFTER!!!!!! R U IN!?!?!?!?!?!?!?!?

I bet you know A is the right answer for all of these. Even if you can understand B and C, did you notice how annoying they are to try to figure out? A, on the other hand, is always easy to read.

A Social Media Story

Sonia posts a picture of herself wearing a brand-new sweater. It's the best sweater ever!

Maria gives it a heart and two thumbs up. Teddy says, "Neat!" The likes keep coming in all afternoon, until Janet comments.

Janet says, "Ew, that sweater is SO UGLY!!!!" Sonia is really upset. She's sad *and* she's mad. Without thinking, she writes back, "Whatever, Janet! Your clothes are ALWAYS UGLY. JUST LIKE YOUR FACE!!!!"

Right away Sonia knows she messed up, but before she can even delete it, Janet writes back and says something even meaner. Then Tanya jumps in, defending Sonia. Then Dawn writes back, defending Sonia.

In no time, everyone is fighting. Over a sweater! It's so silly. Sonia ends up deleting the whole thing.

To avoid social media nightmares like this, you just need to do a few super simple things.

1. Only say things online that you'd say in real life.

2. Only meanies say mean things. If you have something nice to say, share away. Otherwise, keep it to yourself.

3. If someone starts being mean to you online, don't take the low road down to their level (see Tip #19, page 55). Ignore them, block them, or be kind to them. You'll feel better about yourself if you act calm, cool, and collected than if you act like a meanie.

Spelling and grammar count on social media the same way they do in e-mails and texts. DON'T FORGET THAT ALL CAPS MAKES IT SEEM LIKE YOU'RE YELLING!!!!!

Privacy and Oversharing

The Internet is SO BIG. There is so much stuff out there, who is ever going to pay attention to what one kid posts?

The answer is, you don't know who is paying attention. Even if you share something on a private account that only your friends can see, someone could copy it or take a screenshot, and share it on a non-private account. There is no such thing as privacy on the Internet.

That means if you post something gross or embarrassing online, everyone might see it. Imagine you sat on a brownie and it was *hilarious*. I don't think I need to explain why! You take a picture of yourself smiling, wearing your brownie-stained pants, and text it to your friend. If your friend's annoying brother gets his hands on that phone, he might share that picture online. With *everyone*.

To make sure you don't overshare and get embarrassed online, just remember, everything you post or send in a message could get seen by practically the whole world. It will also hang around for a *really* long time.

If you wouldn't want your parents to see something, don't send it. If you wouldn't want bullies to see something, don't send it. Basically, if you wouldn't want the world to see something, don't send it.

DO I KNOW YOU?

If you have social media accounts, you probably get a ton of friend requests. You're a great kid! A lot of those requests come from people you know, but what do you do when you get a friend request from a stranger?

Even if that person looks like another kid your age who you'd be happy to be friends with, you don't really know who is at the other end. The safest thing you can do is only accept requests from people you actually know IRL (in real life). The same goes for messaging.

If you're not sure whether or not you know someone, check out who their friends are. Maybe the picture that came with a friend request looks like that kid from your soccer team. But he's got a ton of frosting on his face from getting hit with birthday cake, and you don't remember his name. You're not sure. If he's friends with half your team, it's probably him. If he doesn't have any friends you know, it's probably not him. Either way, you can ask him about it the next time you have soccer practice, and you can friend request at the same time!

Earphones

We all love to listen to music. Earphones can make it feel like we're at our very own concert. Rock on! But earphones are meant for alone time. If you put them on when you're with other people, they'll think you're not interested in them or don't like them. That sounds rude to me!

Don't forget that people around us can hear what's coming out of our earphones if we have the volume turned way up. When we're in a quiet place like the library or a crowded place like a train, we should keep the volume around the middle. That way we won't make everyone around us listen to our tunes. Remember, thinking about the people around us is the key to great manners!

When we've got our earphones on, it is important to stay aware of what's going on around us. For safety and good manners, we still need to keep an eye out for people who might be trying to get our attention, either by looking up every now and then, or turning the volume down a smidge.

41

Rules for Being Safe Online

It's easy to stay safe online. It's mostly about *not* doing things that could be bad, which, lucky for you, means no extra work!

QUICK TIPS FOR ONLINE SAFETY

✗ **DON'T** talk to strangers.

✗ **DON'T** give out your passwords, address, phone number, or really anything with numbers in it. Same goes for where you go to school, where your parents work, or any other personal information.

✗ **DON'T** send pictures you wouldn't want the world to see.

✗ **DON'T** say things you wouldn't want the world to read.

✗ **DON'T** agree to meet someone you don't know IRL.

There are only two things you actually have to *do* for online safety.

✔ **DO** tell your parents if you ever get a message or see something that makes you uncomfortable.

✔ **DO** make sure all your social media is set to private so only your friends can see what you post.

LET'S REVIEW!

Phones, the Internet and other technology are totally awesome when we are considerate and well-mannered.

★ Try to keep your phone on silent and stay off it while out with family and friends.

★ When answering the phone, be polite and helpful, but stay safe, too.

★ Correct spelling and good grammar are really important in e-mails and text messages. Use acronyms only if everyone knows what you are saying!

★ Don't send texts, make posts, or take pictures if you wouldn't want your parents or the whole world to see them.

★ Don't post any personal information, and check before accepting a friend request.

★ Always check the volume of your earphones and pay attention to your surroundings.

Chapter 6

Parties, Sleepovers, Dances, and Special Occasions

It's party time! Good manners can help you have a fantastic time, because you'll always know the right things to do and say. They also make you a great guest, which means you'll get invited to more stuff like this!

Invitation and RSVP Etiquette

You're having a party. Cool! Sending out invitations gives your guests the details they need to have a great time. An invitation should include these details:

The address where you're partying.

The date and time of the party.

What the party is for. Is it a birthday? Is it a surprise?

What kind of party will it be? Pool party? Bowling party? House party? Slumber party? There are so many kinds of parties! If guests need to bring special supplies—like a swimsuit or a sleeping bag—be sure to let them know.

Is there a theme? If it's a princess party, I don't want to show up in my cowgirl hat!

How you want guests to RSVP. An RSVP is just the fancy way of saying please respond (it stands for *répondez s'il vous plaît* in French).

You got invited to a party. Awesome! When you get an invitation, read the details carefully. Then check with your parents to see if you can go.

Now it's time to RSVP. That's just a fancy way of saying you're going to let someone know whether or not you can go to their party.

An invitation usually tells you how to RSVP. It might be a phone call, an e-mail, or a text message. If it doesn't say, a phone call will do the trick.

The invitation will also tell you when you should RSVP by. Whether you're able to go or not, make sure you let the party planner know by the RSVP date. That part is really important!

Being a Guest

Marco and Raj are both invited to Louis's birthday pool party. They are both *really* excited.

When Marco gets there, he runs straight through the house. He drops his stuff, including the birthday present, in a pile in the backyard and cannonballs into the pool. "Wahoo!" he yells. He cannonballs at least ten more times, yelling each time.

When the birthday cake comes out, he doesn't want to get out of the pool. He's having too much fun! He is hungry though, so once everyone is done singing, he gets out to down a piece of cake as fast as he can. He drops his plate and runs back to the pool while Louis opens his presents. He yells from the pool, "Hey, Louis, my present is over there, near that bush!"

When Raj gets to the party, he's dying to get into the pool. First things first though! He finds the table for the presents and drops off his gift. Then he goes outside to find Louis and wishes him a happy birthday. He also says, "Thanks for inviting me!" to Louis's parents.

Then Raj runs over to the pool and CANNONBALL! He has a great time swimming around. When the cake comes out, he gets out of the pool to sing happy birthday with his friends. He waits until a piece of cake is passed to him. It's so good! He throws out his paper plate. Then he helps pass presents to Louis while Louis opens them. Raj is happy to hand Louis his present, a puzzle of outer space!

Can you guess who got invited to Louis's party the following year?

DOs & DON'Ts > BEING THE BEST GUEST

Whether you're at a party or just going to hang out, you'll be every-one's favorite guest if you follow these simple DOs and DON'Ts.

- ✔ DO make sure you say hello to everyone you see, including your friend's parents and other family members.

- ✔ DO remember the magic words (Tip #1, page 22). Always thank your friend and their parents for invit-ing you to their house, party, or any place you go with them.

- ✔ DO wait your turn for food.

- ✔ DO clean up after yourself.

- ✔ DO ask before using the phone or getting a snack.

★ ★ ★

- ✗ DON'T run around, throw toys, or do anything you aren't allowed to do in your own home.

- ✗ DON'T yell, scream, shout, or make tons of noise.

- ✗ DON'T snoop around in rooms and through people's stuff. You wouldn't want someone going through your games or messing up your art project!

POP QUIZ!

Being the Best Guest

Hanging out with friends at each other's houses can be so much fun! Can you pick out the right thing to do in each situation?

You get to your friend's house and see her mom in the kitchen. You:

- **A.** Walk right past. You're there to see your friend.
- **B.** Say hello.
- **C.** Try to sneak past so you don't bug her.

Your friend has to go do a quick chore. You:

- **A.** Wander around the house while she's busy.
- **B.** Offer to help with the chore.
- **C.** Go through her drawers while she's gone.

You're really thirsty. You:

- **A.** Go to the kitchen to get yourself some juice.
- **B.** Tell your friend you're thirsty and ask if you can have some juice.
- **C.** Complain that no one has given you anything to drink yet.

You and your friends spent the afternoon doing arts and crafts, and now it's time for dinner. You:

- **A.** Rush home with your cool new craft.
- **B.** Help clean up before heading home.
- **C.** Start a new craft because you're having fun.

If you answered all **B**s, you're right! Good manners make it easy to be a good friend and houseguest!

sleepovers

When you sleep over at someone else's house, it's like you get to live with them. Even if it's just for one night. Be sure you bring your toothbrush, clothes to sleep in, and clothes for the next day. A little gift for your hosts (your friend and their parents) will show you have amazing manners. Whether you're going to your best friend's house or a new friend's house, nothing says "Thank you for inviting me!" like some homemade cookies.

At a sleepover, try to go with the flow. Eat the food you're offered. Play the games your friend wants to play. Be friendly to your friend's whole family. If your friend goes to bed at nine, but your normal bedtime is ten, don't make a fuss. Go to bed when they do at nine (and don't say, "That's not how we do it at *my* house.")

Even if it's a sleepover party with lots of kids, be quiet once it gets late. If you get sick, scared, or homesick, your friend's parents will help you out. Don't be afraid to let them know if you're not up to staying the night. If you stay the whole night, be kind and courteous in the morning and don't forget your toothbrush!

Giving Gifts

Believe it or not, giving gifts can make us feel just as good as receiving them. When we're invited to birthday parties, weddings, and showers, it's great manners to bring a gift. If the invitation says not to bring gifts (yes, that really does happen!), a handmade card is a fun way to show we care without ignoring the wish.

When we know we want to give a gift, that can mean a shopping trip. Let your parents know right away if you want to give a gift to someone, so you can be sure to get it in plenty of time for the party.

When picking out gifts, we should think of who the gift is for. What does that person like? Puzzles? Games? Clothes? Horses? Robots? Dinosaurs? Cars? Candy? Spicy food? Dancing? Gift giving gives us the chance to be both kind and creative.

Once we have the gift, it gets wrapped and a card gets taped to the top. Presto! We're perfect gift givers.

Getting Gifts

Getting gifts sounds so exciting! What could possibly go wrong? Most times, it is pure awesome, but if we forget our manners, someone's feelings could get hurt.

When we get gifts, we should thank the giver right away. We should also think of something extra nice to say, like "Wow, this is so cool!" or "I can't wait to try this out!"

If we don't really like a gift or already have something similar, we should tell the giver we hate it and to take it back.

Wait, that doesn't sound nice at all. The giver is definitely going to feel awful if we say that!

Even when we get a gift we don't want, we still should thank the giver and say something kind. The giver is doing something really great for us, and that deserves our thanks. A gift can usually be exchanged if it's unopened. Or we can donate it!

Thank-You Notes

Thank-you notes are a way to show superpower manners. They take no time to write, and they're sure to make someone's day. You should definitely send them when you get a gift, and they're a whole lot easier to write right after you get the gift. Then you don't forget!

You can also send them when someone does something really nice for you. Say your aunt took you to a theme park, went on all the rides with you, and even got you delicious snacks. Sure, you said thank you at the time, but a thank-you note will brighten her day. She may even be more likely to take you somewhere else awesome soon.

The Parts of a
Thank-You Note

You can buy special cards that are made just for saying thanks. Better yet, you can make a thank-you note from scratch. If you do that, you can add stickers, draw pictures, and really make them your own.

Think of the last gift you got, or something really nice that someone did for you. Write that person a thank-you note using the tips from "The Parts of a Thank-You Note." Even if you want to thank someone for something that happened more than one month ago, they will still be very happy to get the note.

Go ahead and try writing a thank-you note right now. After all, there is no time like the *present*!

No matter what kind of note you want to send, all thank-you notes should have a few simple things.

Here's an example of a wonderful, fast, and easy thank-you note:

Dear Uncle Mike,

Thank you for the awesome remote control truck!

I've been racing it around the backyard. Our dog. Jimjam. Loves chasing it almost as much as I love driving it.

I hope you and Aunt Roxy had an awesome time at the Llama show.

Thanks again!

Love,

Felix

Dressing for the Occasion

Jocelyn, Emma, Tyrone, and Mark were all invited to the same wedding. Jocelyn showed up in a cute new dress with stockings and shiny shoes. Tyrone was excited to wear his fancy vest and bowtie, because he didn't get to wear them very often. Jocelyn and Tyrone fit right in with all the people wearing gowns and suits. They didn't think about their clothes all night—except when they got compliments on their outfits—because they had dressed right for the occasion.

Emma didn't like the way her best dress scratched at her neck, and Mark didn't like how his shiny shoes pinched his toes. They both ended up wearing their favorite jeans. Emma wore a sparkly T-shirt, because sparkles are fancy, right? Mark wore a zip-up fleece because he didn't want to get cold. Emma and Mark spent the whole wedding feeling embarrassed because everyone else looked so dressed-up and fancy, while they were just in their regular clothes.

You should dress up for special occasions like weddings, dances, and adult parties. If you do your best to look good, you'll feel good, and the hosts will know you're having a good time, too. And if you get into the spirit of the party, dressing up can be really fun! If you're ever not sure what to wear somewhere, ask your parents for help.

DOs & DON'Ts > PARTIES

It just takes a few simple DOs and DON'Ts to make you a great
party guest!

- ✔ DO RSVP, show up on time, and dress to impress.

- ✔ DO remember the magic words (Tip #1, page 22).

- ✔ DO be nice to *everyone*.

- ✔ DO go along with the games and activities your host
  has planned.

- ✔ DO bring a gift if it's a birthday or wedding party.

- ✔ DO thank the hosts for inviting you.

★ ★ ★

- ✗ DON'T invite other people to go to the party with
  you unless the invitation says you can.

- ✗ DON'T eat more than your fair share.

- ✗ DON'T complain if you don't like something like
  the food or the game everyone is playing.

- ✗ DON'T run around screaming like a maniac
  (especially at adult parties and weddings).

- ✗ DON'T leave the party zone.

- ✗ DON'T make a huge mess.

Knowing manners makes parties and other special occasions
a breeze!

Dances

Going to a dance can be really exciting *and* a little bit scary. Dances are a big sign that you're growing up, and part of growing up is learning the right ways to act in all kinds of exciting, new, and sometimes scary situations. Don't worry! Good manners are here to tell you just what to do!

Dances are special occasions, so you dress up specially just for them. You'll be on your feet a lot, so try to wear shoes that look good and feel good.

There may be a lot of soda and candy around, but don't have too much of the sweet stuff. A lot of sugar can make you act way too silly or even give you a bellyache. If you feel nervous, try to avoid sugary stuff completely, because sweets can make you feel even worse.

It's a *dance* (not a run-around-yelling-free-for-all), so you'll probably want to do some dancing. If you're nervous about dancing with people one-on-one, it's a lot of fun to dance in a group with your friends.

If someone asks you to dance but you don't want to, be polite about saying no. Even if you secretly think that person is kind of gross, a simple "No, thank you," is all you have to say. Remember, everyone has feelings and everyone deserves respect.

If you ask someone to dance and they say no, don't sweat it. You can still have a great time dancing with someone else.

The secret to having a good time at dances, or any other party, is to remember you're the one in charge of you. If you decide to have good manners and a good time, you'll have fun no matter what. You will be proud of yourself and the way you act.

At the Movies with Friends

Everyone loves seeing a movie with friends. It's the best! When we go with a group of our close buds to see a flick, it's easy to let our excitement take over—and forget our manners. But forgetting our manners means we might ruin the movie for the people around us. Not cool!

To make sure everyone in the theater has a good time, *everyone* has to remember to turn off their phones. Even when a phone is on silent, if it lights up because it's ringing, or someone is checking their texts, the other people in the theater will be distracted by the screen. It's a super rude move to be on your phone during a movie. Plus, you'll miss all the good parts!

Talking or even just whispering during a movie is also distracting. People are there to hear the movie—not what other people think about it.

Feet stay on the floor, not on the seats. And no kicking other people's seatbacks.

If we have to make a bathroom trip, being quick and quiet is key. We don't want to block people's view for long as we go past them, and we don't want to miss the movie!

Making the people who work at the theater clean up after us is a rude move. When we leave the theater, we should take our garbage with us, right? Right!

LET'S REVIEW!

Knowing good manners makes parties and other special occasions a breeze.

★ *Invitations have all the information you need to know, but don't forget to RSVP.*

★ *While getting gifts is excellent, giving gifts feels good, too. Don't forget to write a thank-you note.*

★ *Dress up for special occasions like weddings, dances, and adult parties. If you do your best to look good, you'll feel good.*

★ *You should use your manners at the movies, too!*

★ *No matter where you go, if you have good manners you'll be on the right track to have fun.*

Chapter 7

What to Say When . . .
What to Do When . . .

Knowing the right things to do or say in a sticky or sad situation can be tough. Once again, manners to the rescue! This chapter will help you learn extra-special manners that will show the people around that you care.

A Friend Tells You They Failed a Test...

WHAT TO SAY

"That was a tough one! You'll do better next time."

WHAT TO DO

If it's a subject you are good at, offer to help them study for the next one.

You Forgot Someone's Birthday ...

WHAT TO SAY

"Happy belated birthday! I'm sorry I didn't get to talk to you on your birthday. Did you have a good day?"

WHAT TO DO

If it's a close friend, you can try to make it up to them by planning something especially for them.

Your Friend Is Upset Because You Weren't Able to Invite Them to Something . . .

WHAT TO SAY

"I'm sorry I wasn't able to invite you."

WHAT TO DO

Make plans to do something that friend really likes doing, like playing a game together or going to the movies.

A CLassmate AsKs you for Answers on a Test...

WHAT TO SAY

"No way."

WHAT TO DO

Just ignore them. Especially if a bully asks, ignoring them is the best thing you can do.

You See a Friend Stealing, Hitting, or Breaking Someone Else's Stuff...

WHAT TO SAY

"Stop it!"

WHAT TO DO

If your friend is acting like a meanie, you can tell them you are not cool with it. If they don't stop acting like a meanie, you can tell an adult. You should also think about whether you really want to be their friend if they keep acting that way.

YOU KNOW YOUR FRIEND IS LYING TO YOU ABOUT SOMETHING . . .

WHAT TO SAY

" You can always tell me the truth. That's what friends are for."

WHAT TO DO

If your friend is lying because they're afraid the truth will hurt your feelings, or they feel bad about something, give them a break. Let them know you know what's up, without making a huge deal about it. If your friend is lying because they're being a meanie, you can tell them you don't like being treated that way. If they keep up the meanie behavior, you don't have to keep hanging out with them.

You are visiting someone in the Hospital ...

WHAT TO SAY

"I hope you feel better soon."

WHAT TO DO

Bring flowers if possible and imagine how tough it is for the person who has to be there. If you look happy to see that person, you'll really brighten their day.

YOU ARE GOING TO SEE YOUR GRANDMA AND SHE ALWAYS PINCHES YOUR CHEEK...

WHAT TO SAY

"Hi, Grandma! It's great to see you."

WHAT TO DO

Your grandparents and other family members love you and get excited to see you. Even if all those pinches and kisses on your cheeks are annoying, putting up with them can make your family members happy. If you *really* hate it or it's making you feel uncomfortable, tell your mom or dad.

You see a wardrobe malfunction like toilet paper stuck to someone's shoe...

WHAT TO SAY

"Pssst...."

WHAT TO DO

If it's just you two, tell them what's gone wrong without making a big deal about it and embarrassing them. If you're around a bunch of people, take them off to the side and quietly let them know what's going on.

You Use the Bathroom at Someone Else's House and the Toilet Won't Work...

WHAT TO SAY

Find an adult and tell them,

"I'm sorry to bother you, but the toilet isn't working."

WHAT TO DO

You probably will feel a little embarrassed, but these things happen. Just remember, it happens to everyone.

Your Friend Borrowed Something and Hasn't Given It Back...

WHAT TO SAY

"I'd like my toy/game/ book/banana back. Could you please go get it for me?"

WHAT TO DO

Hmm, you probably won't want a used banana back. For the other stuff, you can certainly remind your friend you want your stuff back. Suggest they bring it to school the next day or when they come over to hang out next.

A Friend Tells You Their Parents are Getting Divorced...

WHAT TO SAY

"I'm really sorry! You can come over to my house to hang out whenever you want."

WHAT TO DO

Offer to listen if they want to talk about it. Don't push them to talk about it.

A Friend Has had a Death in Their Family . . .

WHAT TO SAY

"I'm so sorry for your loss."

WHAT TO DO

Offer to listen if they want to talk about it.

someone is making you uncomfortable...

WHAT TO SAY

Depending on what's going on, you can say *"I have to leave"* or if you feel very uncomfortable, you can simply walk away without saying anything.

WHAT TO DO

Walk away and find your friends or an adult you trust. Tell them what happened. If someone is making you feel bad, you don't ever have to apologize for walking away.

You Receive a Gift You're Not Crazy About...

WHAT TO SAY

"Thank you!"

WHAT TO DO

Accept the gift with gratitude and write a thank-you note. You can donate it or offer to let your siblings play with it or use it as much as they like.

Index

About the Author

KATHERINE FLANNERY is a writer and editor with super good manners. Her good manners have helped her run her own business, make lots of friends, and generally get along with people without a lot of drama. She learned it all from her mother, who was the Gibb's Girl of the Year when she graduated from Katharine Gibbs School and has possibly the best manners on the planet. Katherine is excited to pass on to the next generation all the confidence and contentment that comes with good manners.

CPSIA information can be obtained
at www.ICGtesting.com
Printed in the USA
JSHW031636090720
6541JS00004B/62

9 781641 520959